DETAILS

NAME:

ADDRESS:

EMAIL:

WEBSITE:

PHONE: | FAX:

EMERGENCY CONTACT PERSON:

PHONE: | EMAIL:

LOGBOOK DETAILS | COMMENTS

CONTINUED FROM LOG BOOK:

LOG START DATE:

CONTINUED TO LOG BOOK:

LOG END DATE:

CROWN
JOURNALS

CLUE SCORE SHEET

SUSPECTS

A.					
B.					
C.					
D.					
E.					
F.					

WEAPONS

KNIFE					
CANDLESTICK					
REVOLVER					
ROPE					
LEAD PIPE					
WRENCH					

ROOMS

HALL					
LOUNGE					
DINING ROOM					
KITCHEN					
BALL ROOM					
CONSERVATORY					
BILLIARDS ROOM					
LIBRARY					
STUDY					

CLUE SCORE SHEET

SUSPECTS

A.						
B.						
C.						
D.						
E.						
F.						

WEAPONS

KNIFE						
CANDLESTICK						
REVOLVER						
ROPE						
LEAD PIPE						
WRENCH						

ROOMS

HALL						
LOUNGE						
DINING ROOM						
KITCHEN						
BALL ROOM						
CONSERVATORY						
BILLIARDS ROOM						
LIBRARY						
STUDY						

CLUE SCORE SHEET

SUSPECTS

A.						
B.						
C.						
D.						
E.						
F.						

WEAPONS

KNIFE						
CANDLESTICK						
REVOLVER						
ROPE						
LEAD PIPE						
WRENCH						

ROOMS

HALL						
LOUNGE						
DINING ROOM						
KITCHEN						
BALL ROOM						
CONSERVATORY						
BILLIARDS ROOM						
LIBRARY						
STUDY						

CLUE SCORE SHEET

SUSPECTS

A.						
B.						
C.						
D.						
E.						
F.						

WEAPONS

KNIFE						
CANDLESTICK						
REVOLVER						
ROPE						
LEAD PIPE						
WRENCH						

ROOMS

HALL						
LOUNGE						
DINING ROOM						
KITCHEN						
BALL ROOM						
CONSERVATORY						
BILLIARDS ROOM						
LIBRARY						
STUDY						

CLUE SCORE SHEET

SUSPECTS

A.						
B.						
C.						
D.						
E.						
F.						

WEAPONS

KNIFE						
CANDLESTICK						
REVOLVER						
ROPE						
LEAD PIPE						
WRENCH						

ROOMS

HALL						
LOUNGE						
DINING ROOM						
KITCHEN						
BALL ROOM						
CONSERVATORY						
BILLIARDS ROOM						
LIBRARY						
STUDY						

CLUE SCORE SHEET

SUSPECTS

A.						
B.						
C.						
D.						
E.						
F.						

WEAPONS

KNIFE						
CANDLESTICK						
REVOLVER						
ROPE						
LEAD PIPE						
WRENCH						
OTHER						
OTHER						

ROOMS

HALL						
LOUNGE						
DINING ROOM						
KITCHEN						
BALL ROOM						
CONSERVATORY						
BILLIARDS ROOM						
LIBRARY						
STUDY						
OTHER						
OTHER						

CLUE SCORE SHEET

SUSPECTS

A.					
B.					
C.					
D.					
E.					
F.					

WEAPONS

KNIFE					
CANDLESTICK					
REVOLVER					
ROPE					
LEAD PIPE					
WRENCH					

ROOMS

HALL					
LOUNGE					
DINING ROOM					
KITCHEN					
BALL ROOM					
CONSERVATORY					
BILLIARDS ROOM					
LIBRARY					
STUDY					

CLUE SCORE SHEET

SUSPECTS

A.					
B.					
C.					
D.					
E.					
F.					

WEAPONS

KNIFE					
CANDLESTICK					
REVOLVER					
ROPE					
LEAD PIPE					
WRENCH					

ROOMS

HALL					
LOUNGE					
DINING ROOM					
KITCHEN					
BALL ROOM					
CONSERVATORY					
BILLIARDS ROOM					
LIBRARY					
STUDY					

CLUE SCORE SHEET

SUSPECTS

A.						
B.						
C.						
D.						
E.						
F.						

WEAPONS

KNIFE						
CANDLESTICK						
REVOLVER						
ROPE						
LEAD PIPE						
WRENCH						

ROOMS

HALL						
LOUNGE						
DINING ROOM						
KITCHEN						
BALL ROOM						
CONSERVATORY						
BILLIARDS ROOM						
LIBRARY						
STUDY						

CLUE SCORE SHEET

SUSPECTS

A.						
B.						
C.						
D.						
E.						
F.						

WEAPONS

KNIFE						
CANDLESTICK						
REVOLVER						
ROPE						
LEAD PIPE						
WRENCH						
OTHER						
OTHER						

ROOMS

HALL						
LOUNGE						
DINING ROOM						
KITCHEN						
BALL ROOM						
CONSERVATORY						
BILLIARDS ROOM						
LIBRARY						
STUDY						
OTHER						
OTHER						

CLUE SCORE SHEET

SUSPECTS

A.					
B.					
C.					
D.					
E.					
F.					

WEAPONS

KNIFE					
CANDLESTICK					
REVOLVER					
ROPE					
LEAD PIPE					
WRENCH					

ROOMS

HALL					
LOUNGE					
DINING ROOM					
KITCHEN					
BALL ROOM					
CONSERVATORY					
BILLIARDS ROOM					
LIBRARY					
STUDY					

CLUE SCORE SHEET

SUSPECTS

A.					
B.					
C.					
D.					
E.					
F.					

WEAPONS

KNIFE					
CANDLESTICK					
REVOLVER					
ROPE					
LEAD PIPE					
WRENCH					

ROOMS

HALL					
LOUNGE					
DINING ROOM					
KITCHEN					
BALL ROOM					
CONSERVATORY					
BILLIARDS ROOM					
LIBRARY					
STUDY					

CLUE SCORE SHEET

A.					
B.					
C.					
D.					
E.					
F.					

KNIFE					
CANDLESTICK					
REVOLVER					
ROPE					
LEAD PIPE					
WRENCH					

HALL					
LOUNGE					
DINING ROOM					
KITCHEN					
BALL ROOM					
CONSERVATORY					
BILLIARDS ROOM					
LIBRARY					
STUDY					

CLUE SCORE SHEET

SUSPECTS

A.						
B.						
C.						
D.						
E.						
F.						

WEAPONS

KNIFE						
CANDLESTICK						
REVOLVER						
ROPE						
LEAD PIPE						
WRENCH						
OTHER						
OTHER						

ROOMS

HALL						
LOUNGE						
DINING ROOM						
KITCHEN						
BALL ROOM						
CONSERVATORY						
BILLIARDS ROOM						
LIBRARY						
STUDY						
OTHER						
OTHER						

CLUE SCORE SHEET

A.					
B.					
C.					
D.					
E.					
F.					

KNIFE					
CANDLESTICK					
REVOLVER					
ROPE					
LEAD PIPE					
WRENCH					

HALL					
LOUNGE					
DINING ROOM					
KITCHEN					
BALL ROOM					
CONSERVATORY					
BILLIARDS ROOM					
LIBRARY					
STUDY					

CLUE SCORE SHEET

SUSPECTS

A.						
B.						
C.						
D.						
E.						
F.						

WEAPONS

KNIFE						
CANDLESTICK						
REVOLVER						
ROPE						
LEAD PIPE						
WRENCH						

ROOMS

HALL						
LOUNGE						
DINING ROOM						
KITCHEN						
BALL ROOM						
CONSERVATORY						
BILLIARDS ROOM						
LIBRARY						
STUDY						

CLUE SCORE SHEET

SUSPECTS

A.					
B.					
C.					
D.					
E.					
F.					

WEAPONS

KNIFE					
CANDLESTICK					
REVOLVER					
ROPE					
LEAD PIPE					
WRENCH					

ROOMS

HALL					
LOUNGE					
DINING ROOM					
KITCHEN					
BALL ROOM					
CONSERVATORY					
BILLIARDS ROOM					
LIBRARY					
STUDY					

CLUE SCORE SHEET

SUSPECTS

A.						
B.						
C.						
D.						
E.						
F.						

WEAPONS

KNIFE						
CANDLESTICK						
REVOLVER						
ROPE						
LEAD PIPE						
WRENCH						
OTHER						
OTHER						

ROOMS

HALL						
LOUNGE						
DINING ROOM						
KITCHEN						
BALL ROOM						
CONSERVATORY						
BILLIARDS ROOM						
LIBRARY						
STUDY						
OTHER						
OTHER						

CLUE SCORE SHEET

SUSPECTS

A.					
B.					
C.					
D.					
E.					
F.					

WEAPONS

KNIFE					
CANDLESTICK					
REVOLVER					
ROPE					
LEAD PIPE					
WRENCH					

ROOMS

HALL					
LOUNGE					
DINING ROOM					
KITCHEN					
BALL ROOM					
CONSERVATORY					
BILLIARDS ROOM					
LIBRARY					
STUDY					

CLUE SCORE SHEET

SUSPECTS

A.					
B.					
C.					
D.					
E.					
F.					

WEAPONS

KNIFE					
CANDLESTICK					
REVOLVER					
ROPE					
LEAD PIPE					
WRENCH					

ROOMS

HALL					
LOUNGE					
DINING ROOM					
KITCHEN					
BALL ROOM					
CONSERVATORY					
BILLIARDS ROOM					
LIBRARY					
STUDY					

CLUE SCORE SHEET

SUSPECTS

A.					
B.					
C.					
D.					
E.					
F.					

WEAPONS

KNIFE				
CANDLESTICK				
REVOLVER				
ROPE				
LEAD PIPE				
WRENCH				

ROOMS

HALL				
LOUNGE				
DINING ROOM				
KITCHEN				
BALL ROOM				
CONSERVATORY				
BILLIARDS ROOM				
LIBRARY				
STUDY				

CLUE SCORE SHEET

SUSPECTS

A.						
B.						
C.						
D.						
E.						
F.						

WEAPONS

KNIFE						
CANDLESTICK						
REVOLVER						
ROPE						
LEAD PIPE						
WRENCH						

ROOMS

HALL						
LOUNGE						
DINING ROOM						
KITCHEN						
BALL ROOM						
CONSERVATORY						
BILLIARDS ROOM						
LIBRARY						
STUDY						

CLUE SCORE SHEET

SUSPECTS

A.					
B.					
C.					
D.					
E.					
F.					

WEAPONS

KNIFE					
CANDLESTICK					
REVOLVER					
ROPE					
LEAD PIPE					
WRENCH					

ROOMS

HALL					
LOUNGE					
DINING ROOM					
KITCHEN					
BALL ROOM					
CONSERVATORY					
BILLIARDS ROOM					
LIBRARY					
STUDY					

CLUE SCORE SHEET

SUSPECTS

A.						
B.						
C.						
D.						
E.						
F.						

WEAPONS

KNIFE						
CANDLESTICK						
REVOLVER						
ROPE						
LEAD PIPE						
WRENCH						

ROOMS

HALL						
LOUNGE						
DINING ROOM						
KITCHEN						
BALL ROOM						
CONSERVATORY						
BILLIARDS ROOM						
LIBRARY						
STUDY						

CLUE SCORE SHEET

SUSPECTS

A.					
B.					
C.					
D.					
E.					
F.					

WEAPONS

KNIFE					
CANDLESTICK					
REVOLVER					
ROPE					
LEAD PIPE					
WRENCH					

ROOMS

HALL					
LOUNGE					
DINING ROOM					
KITCHEN					
BALL ROOM					
CONSERVATORY					
BILLIARDS ROOM					
LIBRARY					
STUDY					

CLUE SCORE SHEET

SUSPECTS

A.						
B.						
C.						
D.						
E.						
F.						

WEAPONS

KNIFE						
CANDLESTICK						
REVOLVER						
ROPE						
LEAD PIPE						
WRENCH						
OTHER						
OTHER						

ROOMS

HALL						
LOUNGE						
DINING ROOM						
KITCHEN						
BALL ROOM						
CONSERVATORY						
BILLIARDS ROOM						
LIBRARY						
STUDY						
OTHER						
OTHER						

CLUE SCORE SHEET

SUSPECTS

A.					
B.					
C.					
D.					
E.					
F.					

WEAPONS

KNIFE					
CANDLESTICK					
REVOLVER					
ROPE					
LEAD PIPE					
WRENCH					

ROOMS

HALL					
LOUNGE					
DINING ROOM					
KITCHEN					
BALL ROOM					
CONSERVATORY					
BILLIARDS ROOM					
LIBRARY					
STUDY					

CLUE SCORE SHEET

SUSPECTS

A.						
B.						
C.						
D.						
E.						
F.						

WEAPONS

KNIFE						
CANDLESTICK						
REVOLVER						
ROPE						
LEAD PIPE						
WRENCH						

ROOMS

HALL						
LOUNGE						
DINING ROOM						
KITCHEN						
BALL ROOM						
CONSERVATORY						
BILLIARDS ROOM						
LIBRARY						
STUDY						

CLUE SCORE SHEET

SUSPECTS

A.					
B.					
C.					
D.					
E.					
F.					

WEAPONS

KNIFE					
CANDLESTICK					
REVOLVER					
ROPE					
LEAD PIPE					
WRENCH					

ROOMS

HALL					
LOUNGE					
DINING ROOM					
KITCHEN					
BALL ROOM					
CONSERVATORY					
BILLIARDS ROOM					
LIBRARY					
STUDY					

CLUE SCORE SHEET

SUSPECTS

A.					
B.					
C.					
D.					
E.					
F.					

WEAPONS

KNIFE					
CANDLESTICK					
REVOLVER					
ROPE					
LEAD PIPE					
WRENCH					
OTHER					
OTHER					

ROOMS

HALL					
LOUNGE					
DINING ROOM					
KITCHEN					
BALL ROOM					
CONSERVATORY					
BILLIARDS ROOM					
LIBRARY					
STUDY					
OTHER					
OTHER					

CLUE SCORE SHEET

A.					
B.					
C.					
D.					
E.					
F.					

KNIFE					
CANDLESTICK					
REVOLVER					
ROPE					
LEAD PIPE					
WRENCH					

HALL					
LOUNGE					
DINING ROOM					
KITCHEN					
BALL ROOM					
CONSERVATORY					
BILLIARDS ROOM					
LIBRARY					
STUDY					

CLUE SCORE SHEET

SUSPECTS

A.					
B.					
C.					
D.					
E.					
F.					

WEAPONS

KNIFE					
CANDLESTICK					
REVOLVER					
ROPE					
LEAD PIPE					
WRENCH					

ROOMS

HALL					
LOUNGE					
DINING ROOM					
KITCHEN					
BALL ROOM					
CONSERVATORY					
BILLIARDS ROOM					
LIBRARY					
STUDY					

CLUE SCORE SHEET

SUSPECTS

A.					
B.					
C.					
D.					
E.					
F.					

WEAPONS

KNIFE					
CANDLESTICK					
REVOLVER					
ROPE					
LEAD PIPE					
WRENCH					

ROOMS

HALL					
LOUNGE					
DINING ROOM					
KITCHEN					
BALL ROOM					
CONSERVATORY					
BILLIARDS ROOM					
LIBRARY					
STUDY					

CLUE SCORE SHEET

SUSPECTS

A.					
B.					
C.					
D.					
E.					
F.					

WEAPONS

KNIFE					
CANDLESTICK					
REVOLVER					
ROPE					
LEAD PIPE					
WRENCH					

ROOMS

HALL					
LOUNGE					
DINING ROOM					
KITCHEN					
BALL ROOM					
CONSERVATORY					
BILLIARDS ROOM					
LIBRARY					
STUDY					

CLUE SCORE SHEET

A.					
B.					
C.					
D.					
E.					
F.					

KNIFE					
CANDLESTICK					
REVOLVER					
ROPE					
LEAD PIPE					
WRENCH					

HALL					
LOUNGE					
DINING ROOM					
KITCHEN					
BALL ROOM					
CONSERVATORY					
BILLIARDS ROOM					
LIBRARY					
STUDY					

CLUE SCORE SHEET

SUSPECTS

A.					
B.					
C.					
D.					
E.					
F.					

WEAPONS

KNIFE					
CANDLESTICK					
REVOLVER					
ROPE					
LEAD PIPE					
WRENCH					

ROOMS

HALL					
LOUNGE					
DINING ROOM					
KITCHEN					
BALL ROOM					
CONSERVATORY					
BILLIARDS ROOM					
LIBRARY					
STUDY					

CLUE SCORE SHEET

SUSPECTS

A.					
B.					
C.					
D.					
E.					
F.					

WEAPONS

KNIFE					
CANDLESTICK					
REVOLVER					
ROPE					
LEAD PIPE					
WRENCH					

ROOMS

HALL					
LOUNGE					
DINING ROOM					
KITCHEN					
BALL ROOM					
CONSERVATORY					
BILLIARDS ROOM					
LIBRARY					
STUDY					

CLUE SCORE SHEET

SUSPECTS

A.					
B.					
C.					
D.					
E.					
F.					

WEAPONS

KNIFE					
CANDLESTICK					
REVOLVER					
ROPE					
LEAD PIPE					
WRENCH					

ROOMS

HALL					
LOUNGE					
DINING ROOM					
KITCHEN					
BALL ROOM					
CONSERVATORY					
BILLIARDS ROOM					
LIBRARY					
STUDY					

CLUE SCORE SHEET

SUSPECTS

A.					
B.					
C.					
D.					
E.					
F.					

WEAPONS

KNIFE					
CANDLESTICK					
REVOLVER					
ROPE					
LEAD PIPE					
WRENCH					

ROOMS

HALL					
LOUNGE					
DINING ROOM					
KITCHEN					
BALL ROOM					
CONSERVATORY					
BILLIARDS ROOM					
LIBRARY					
STUDY					

CLUE SCORE SHEET

SUSPECTS

A.					
B.					
C.					
D.					
E.					
F.					

WEAPONS

KNIFE					
CANDLESTICK					
REVOLVER					
ROPE					
LEAD PIPE					
WRENCH					

ROOMS

HALL					
LOUNGE					
DINING ROOM					
KITCHEN					
BALL ROOM					
CONSERVATORY					
BILLIARDS ROOM					
LIBRARY					
STUDY					

CLUE SCORE SHEET

SUSPECTS

A.					
B.					
C.					
D.					
E.					
F.					

WEAPONS

KNIFE					
CANDLESTICK					
REVOLVER					
ROPE					
LEAD PIPE					
WRENCH					

ROOMS

HALL					
LOUNGE					
DINING ROOM					
KITCHEN					
BALL ROOM					
CONSERVATORY					
BILLIARDS ROOM					
LIBRARY					
STUDY					

CLUE SCORE SHEET

SUPECTS

A.						
B.						
C.						
D.						
E.						
F.						

WEAPONS

KNIFE						
CANDLESTICK						
REVOLVER						
ROPE						
LEAD PIPE						
WRENCH						

ROOMS

HALL						
LOUNGE						
DINING ROOM						
KITCHEN						
BALL ROOM						
CONSERVATORY						
BILLIARDS ROOM						
LIBRARY						
STUDY						

CLUE SCORE SHEET

SUSPECTS

A.					
B.					
C.					
D.					
E.					
F.					

WEAPONS

KNIFE					
CANDLESTICK					
REVOLVER					
ROPE					
LEAD PIPE					
WRENCH					

ROOMS

HALL					
LOUNGE					
DINING ROOM					
KITCHEN					
BALL ROOM					
CONSERVATORY					
BILLIARDS ROOM					
LIBRARY					
STUDY					

CLUE SCORE SHEET

SUSPECTS

A.					
B.					
C.					
D.					
E.					
F.					

WEAPONS

KNIFE					
CANDLESTICK					
REVOLVER					
ROPE					
LEAD PIPE					
WRENCH					

ROOMS

HALL					
LOUNGE					
DINING ROOM					
KITCHEN					
BALL ROOM					
CONSERVATORY					
BILLIARDS ROOM					
LIBRARY					
STUDY					

CLUE SCORE SHEET

SUSPECTS

A.					
B.					
C.					
D.					
E.					
F.					

WEAPONS

KNIFE					
CANDLESTICK					
REVOLVER					
ROPE					
LEAD PIPE					
WRENCH					

ROOMS

HALL					
LOUNGE					
DINING ROOM					
KITCHEN					
BALL ROOM					
CONSERVATORY					
BILLIARDS ROOM					
LIBRARY					
STUDY					

CLUE SCORE SHEET

SUSPECTS

A.						
B.						
C.						
D.						
E.						
F.						

WEAPONS

KNIFE						
CANDLESTICK						
REVOLVER						
ROPE						
LEAD PIPE						
WRENCH						

ROOMS

HALL						
LOUNGE						
DINING ROOM						
KITCHEN						
BALL ROOM						
CONSERVATORY						
BILLIARDS ROOM						
LIBRARY						
STUDY						

CLUE SCORE SHEET

SUSPECTS

A.					
B.					
C.					
D.					
E.					
F.					

WEAPONS

KNIFE					
CANDLESTICK					
REVOLVER					
ROPE					
LEAD PIPE					
WRENCH					

ROOMS

HALL					
LOUNGE					
DINING ROOM					
KITCHEN					
BALL ROOM					
CONSERVATORY					
BILLIARDS ROOM					
LIBRARY					
STUDY					

CLUE SCORE SHEET

SUSPECTS

A.					
B.					
C.					
D.					
E.					
F.					

WEAPONS

KNIFE					
CANDLESTICK					
REVOLVER					
ROPE					
LEAD PIPE					
WRENCH					

ROOMS

HALL					
LOUNGE					
DINING ROOM					
KITCHEN					
BALL ROOM					
CONSERVATORY					
BILLIARDS ROOM					
LIBRARY					
STUDY					

CLUE SCORE SHEET

SUSPECTS

A.						
B.						
C.						
D.						
E.						
F.						

WEAPONS

KNIFE						
CANDLESTICK						
REVOLVER						
ROPE						
LEAD PIPE						
WRENCH						

ROOMS

HALL						
LOUNGE						
DINING ROOM						
KITCHEN						
BALL ROOM						
CONSERVATORY						
BILLIARDS ROOM						
LIBRARY						
STUDY						

CLUE SCORE SHEET

SUSPECTS

A.					
B.					
C.					
D.					
E.					
F.					

WEAPONS

KNIFE					
CANDLESTICK					
REVOLVER					
ROPE					
LEAD PIPE					
WRENCH					

ROOMS

HALL					
LOUNGE					
DINING ROOM					
KITCHEN					
BALL ROOM					
CONSERVATORY					
BILLIARDS ROOM					
LIBRARY					
STUDY					

CLUE SCORE SHEET

SUSPECTS

A.					
B.					
C.					
D.					
E.					
F.					

WEAPONS

KNIFE					
CANDLESTICK					
REVOLVER					
ROPE					
LEAD PIPE					
WRENCH					

ROOMS

HALL					
LOUNGE					
DINING ROOM					
KITCHEN					
BALL ROOM					
CONSERVATORY					
BILLIARDS ROOM					
LIBRARY					
STUDY					

CLUE SCORE SHEET

SUSPECTS

A.						
B.						
C.						
D.						
E.						
F.						

WEAPONS

KNIFE						
CANDLESTICK						
REVOLVER						
ROPE						
LEAD PIPE						
WRENCH						

ROOMS

HALL						
LOUNGE						
DINING ROOM						
KITCHEN						
BALL ROOM						
CONSERVATORY						
BILLIARDS ROOM						
LIBRARY						
STUDY						

CLUE SCORE SHEET

SUSPECTS

A.					
B.					
C.					
D.					
E.					
F.					

WEAPONS

KNIFE					
CANDLESTICK					
REVOLVER					
ROPE					
LEAD PIPE					
WRENCH					

ROOMS

HALL					
LOUNGE					
DINING ROOM					
KITCHEN					
BALL ROOM					
CONSERVATORY					
BILLIARDS ROOM					
LIBRARY					
STUDY					

CLUE SCORE SHEET

SUSPECTS

A.					
B.					
C.					
D.					
E.					
F.					

WEAPONS

KNIFE					
CANDLESTICK					
REVOLVER					
ROPE					
LEAD PIPE					
WRENCH					

ROOMS

HALL					
LOUNGE					
DINING ROOM					
KITCHEN					
BALL ROOM					
CONSERVATORY					
BILLIARDS ROOM					
LIBRARY					
STUDY					

CLUE SCORE SHEET

SUSPECTS

A.					
B.					
C.					
D.					
E.					
F.					

WEAPONS

KNIFE					
CANDLESTICK					
REVOLVER					
ROPE					
LEAD PIPE					
WRENCH					

ROOMS

HALL					
LOUNGE					
DINING ROOM					
KITCHEN					
BALL ROOM					
CONSERVATORY					
BILLIARDS ROOM					
LIBRARY					
STUDY					

CLUE SCORE SHEET

SUSPECTS

A.					
B.					
C.					
D.					
E.					
F.					

WEAPONS

KNIFE					
CANDLESTICK					
REVOLVER					
ROPE					
LEAD PIPE					
WRENCH					

ROOMS

HALL					
LOUNGE					
DINING ROOM					
KITCHEN					
BALL ROOM					
CONSERVATORY					
BILLIARDS ROOM					
LIBRARY					
STUDY					

CLUE SCORE SHEET

SUSPECTS

A.					
B.					
C.					
D.					
E.					
F.					

WEAPONS

KNIFE					
CANDLESTICK					
REVOLVER					
ROPE					
LEAD PIPE					
WRENCH					

ROOMS

HALL					
LOUNGE					
DINING ROOM					
KITCHEN					
BALL ROOM					
CONSERVATORY					
BILLIARDS ROOM					
LIBRARY					
STUDY					

CLUE SCORE SHEET

SUSPECTS

A.						
B.						
C.						
D.						
E.						
F.						

WEAPONS

KNIFE						
CANDLESTICK						
REVOLVER						
ROPE						
LEAD PIPE						
WRENCH						

ROOMS

HALL						
LOUNGE						
DINING ROOM						
KITCHEN						
BALL ROOM						
CONSERVATORY						
BILLIARDS ROOM						
LIBRARY						
STUDY						

CLUE SCORE SHEET

A.					
B.					
C.					
D.					
E.					
F.					

KNIFE					
CANDLESTICK					
REVOLVER					
ROPE					
LEAD PIPE					
WRENCH					

HALL					
LOUNGE					
DINING ROOM					
KITCHEN					
BALL ROOM					
CONSERVATORY					
BILLIARDS ROOM					
LIBRARY					
STUDY					

CLUE SCORE SHEET

SUSPECTS

A.					
B.					
C.					
D.					
E.					
F.					

WEAPONS

KNIFE					
CANDLESTICK					
REVOLVER					
ROPE					
LEAD PIPE					
WRENCH					

ROOMS

HALL					
LOUNGE					
DINING ROOM					
KITCHEN					
BALL ROOM					
CONSERVATORY					
BILLIARDS ROOM					
LIBRARY					
STUDY					

CLUE SCORE SHEET

SUSPECTS

A.					
B.					
C.					
D.					
E.					
F.					

WEAPONS

KNIFE					
CANDLESTICK					
REVOLVER					
ROPE					
LEAD PIPE					
WRENCH					

ROOMS

HALL					
LOUNGE					
DINING ROOM					
KITCHEN					
BALL ROOM					
CONSERVATORY					
BILLIARDS ROOM					
LIBRARY					
STUDY					

CLUE SCORE SHEET

SUSPECTS

A.						
B.						
C.						
D.						
E.						
F.						

WEAPONS

KNIFE						
CANDLESTICK						
REVOLVER						
ROPE						
LEAD PIPE						
WRENCH						

ROOMS

HALL						
LOUNGE						
DINING ROOM						
KITCHEN						
BALL ROOM						
CONSERVATORY						
BILLIARDS ROOM						
LIBRARY						
STUDY						

CLUE SCORE SHEET

SUSPECTS

A.					
B.					
C.					
D.					
E.					
F.					

WEAPONS

KNIFE					
CANDLESTICK					
REVOLVER					
ROPE					
LEAD PIPE					
WRENCH					

ROOMS

HALL					
LOUNGE					
DINING ROOM					
KITCHEN					
BALL ROOM					
CONSERVATORY					
BILLIARDS ROOM					
LIBRARY					
STUDY					

CLUE SCORE SHEET

SUSPECTS

A.					
B.					
C.					
D.					
E.					
F.					

WEAPONS

KNIFE					
CANDLESTICK					
REVOLVER					
ROPE					
LEAD PIPE					
WRENCH					

ROOMS

HALL					
LOUNGE					
DINING ROOM					
KITCHEN					
BALL ROOM					
CONSERVATORY					
BILLIARDS ROOM					
LIBRARY					
STUDY					

CLUE SCORE SHEET

SUSPECTS

A						
B.						
C.						
D.						
E.						
F.						

WEAPONS

KNIFE						
CANDLESTICK						
REVOLVER						
ROPE						
LEAD PIPE						
WRENCH						

ROOMS

HALL						
LOUNGE						
DINING ROOM						
KITCHEN						
BALL ROOM						
CONSERVATORY						
BILLIARDS ROOM						
LIBRARY						
STUDY						

CLUE SCORE SHEET

SUSPECTS

A.						
B.						
C.						
D.						
E.						
F.						

WEAPONS

KNIFE						
CANDLESTICK						
REVOLVER						
ROPE						
LEAD PIPE						
WRENCH						

ROOMS

HALL						
LOUNGE						
DINING ROOM						
KITCHEN						
BALL ROOM						
CONSERVATORY						
BILLIARDS ROOM						
LIBRARY						
STUDY						

CLUE SCORE SHEET

SUSPECTS						
A.						
B.						
C.						
D.						
E.						
F.						

WEAPONS						
KNIFE						
CANDLESTICK						
REVOLVER						
ROPE						
LEAD PIPE						
WRENCH						

ROOMS						
HALL						
LOUNGE						
DINING ROOM						
KITCHEN						
BALL ROOM						
CONSERVATORY						
BILLIARDS ROOM						
LIBRARY						
STUDY						

CLUE SCORE SHEET

SUSPECTS

A.					
B.					
C.					
D.					
E.					
F.					

WEAPONS

KNIFE					
CANDLESTICK					
REVOLVER					
ROPE					
LEAD PIPE					
WRENCH					

ROOMS

HALL					
LOUNGE					
DINING ROOM					
KITCHEN					
BALL ROOM					
CONSERVATORY					
BILLIARDS ROOM					
LIBRARY					
STUDY					

CLUE SCORE SHEET

SUSPECTS

A.					
B.					
C.					
D.					
E.					
F.					

WEAPONS

KNIFE					
CANDLESTICK					
REVOLVER					
ROPE					
LEAD PIPE					
WRENCH					

ROOMS

HALL					
LOUNGE					
DINING ROOM					
KITCHEN					
BALL ROOM					
CONSERVATORY					
BILLIARDS ROOM					
LIBRARY					
STUDY					

CLUE SCORE SHEET

SUSPECTS

A.					
B.					
C.					
D.					
E.					
F.					

WEAPONS

KNIFE					
CANDLESTICK					
REVOLVER					
ROPE					
LEAD PIPE					
WRENCH					

ROOMS

HALL					
LOUNGE					
DINING ROOM					
KITCHEN					
BALL ROOM					
CONSERVATORY					
BILLIARDS ROOM					
LIBRARY					
STUDY					

CLUE SCORE SHEET

SUSPECTS

A.					
B.					
C.					
D.					
E.					
F.					

WEAPONS

KNIFE					
CANDLESTICK					
REVOLVER					
ROPE					
LEAD PIPE					
WRENCH					

ROOMS

HALL					
LOUNGE					
DINING ROOM					
KITCHEN					
BALL ROOM					
CONSERVATORY					
BILLIARDS ROOM					
LIBRARY					
STUDY					

CLUE SCORE SHEET

SUSPECTS

A.					
B.					
C.					
D.					
E.					
F.					

WEAPONS

KNIFE					
CANDLESTICK					
REVOLVER					
ROPE					
LEAD PIPE					
WRENCH					

ROOMS

HALL					
LOUNGE					
DINING ROOM					
KITCHEN					
BALL ROOM					
CONSERVATORY					
BILLIARDS ROOM					
LIBRARY					
STUDY					

CLUE SCORE SHEET

SUSPECTS

A.					
B.					
C.					
D.					
E.					
F.					

WEAPONS

KNIFE				
CANDLESTICK				
REVOLVER				
ROPE				
LEAD PIPE				
WRENCH				

ROOMS

HALL				
LOUNGE				
DINING ROOM				
KITCHEN				
BALL ROOM				
CONSERVATORY				
BILLIARDS ROOM				
LIBRARY				
STUDY				

CLUE SCORE SHEET

SUSPECTS

A.					
B.					
C.					
D.					
E.					
F.					

WEAPONS

KNIFE					
CANDLESTICK					
REVOLVER					
ROPE					
LEAD PIPE					
WRENCH					

ROOMS

HALL					
LOUNGE					
DINING ROOM					
KITCHEN					
BALL ROOM					
CONSERVATORY					
BILLIARDS ROOM					
LIBRARY					
STUDY					

CLUE SCORE SHEET

A.					
B.					
C.					
D.					
E.					
F.					

KNIFE					
CANDLESTICK					
REVOLVER					
ROPE					
LEAD PIPE					
WRENCH					

HALL					
LOUNGE					
DINING ROOM					
KITCHEN					
BALL ROOM					
CONSERVATORY					
BILLIARDS ROOM					
LIBRARY					
STUDY					

CLUE SCORE SHEET

SUSPECTS

A.					
B.					
C.					
D.					
E.					
F.					

WEAPONS

KNIFE					
CANDLESTICK					
REVOLVER					
ROPE					
LEAD PIPE					
WRENCH					

ROOMS

HALL					
LOUNGE					
DINING ROOM					
KITCHEN					
BALL ROOM					
CONSERVATORY					
BILLIARDS ROOM					
LIBRARY					
STUDY					

CLUE SCORE SHEET

SUSPECTS

A.					
B.					
C.					
D.					
E.					
F.					

WEAPONS

KNIFE					
CANDLESTICK					
REVOLVER					
ROPE					
LEAD PIPE					
WRENCH					

ROOMS

HALL					
LOUNGE					
DINING ROOM					
KITCHEN					
BALL ROOM					
CONSERVATORY					
BILLIARDS ROOM					
LIBRARY					
STUDY					

CLUE SCORE SHEET

SUSPECTS

A.					
B.					
C.					
D.					
E.					
F.					

WEAPONS

KNIFE					
CANDLESTICK					
REVOLVER					
ROPE					
LEAD PIPE					
WRENCH					

ROOMS

HALL					
LOUNGE					
DINING ROOM					
KITCHEN					
BALL ROOM					
CONSERVATORY					
BILLIARDS ROOM					
LIBRARY					
STUDY					

CLUE SCORE SHEET

A.					
B.					
C.					
D.					
E.					
F.					

KNIFE					
CANDLESTICK					
REVOLVER					
ROPE					
LEAD PIPE					
WRENCH					

HALL					
LOUNGE					
DINING ROOM					
KITCHEN					
BALL ROOM					
CONSERVATORY					
BILLIARDS ROOM					
LIBRARY					
STUDY					

CLUE SCORE SHEET

SUSPECTS

A.					
B.					
C.					
D.					
E.					
F.					

WEAPONS

KNIFE					
CANDLESTICK					
REVOLVER					
ROPE					
LEAD PIPE					
WRENCH					

ROOMS

HALL					
LOUNGE					
DINING ROOM					
KITCHEN					
BALL ROOM					
CONSERVATORY					
BILLIARDS ROOM					
LIBRARY					
STUDY					

CLUE SCORE SHEET

SUSPECTS

A.					
B.					
C.					
D.					
E.					
F.					

WEAPONS

KNIFE					
CANDLESTICK					
REVOLVER					
ROPE					
LEAD PIPE					
WRENCH					

ROOMS

HALL					
LOUNGE					
DINING ROOM					
KITCHEN					
BALL ROOM					
CONSERVATORY					
BILLIARDS ROOM					
LIBRARY					
STUDY					

CLUE SCORE SHEET

SUSPECTS

A.					
B.					
C.					
D.					
E.					
F.					

WEAPONS

KNIFE					
CANDLESTICK					
REVOLVER					
ROPE					
LEAD PIPE					
WRENCH					

ROOMS

HALL					
LOUNGE					
DINING ROOM					
KITCHEN					
BALL ROOM					
CONSERVATORY					
BILLIARDS ROOM					
LIBRARY					
STUDY					

CLUE SCORE SHEET

SUSPECTS

A.						
B.						
C.						
D.						
E.						
F.						

WEAPONS

KNIFE					
CANDLESTICK					
REVOLVER					
ROPE					
LEAD PIPE					
WRENCH					

ROOMS

HALL					
LOUNGE					
DINING ROOM					
KITCHEN					
BALL ROOM					
CONSERVATORY					
BILLIARDS ROOM					
LIBRARY					
STUDY					

CLUE SCORE SHEET

SUSPECTS

A.					
B.					
C.					
D.					
E.					
F.					

WEAPONS

KNIFE					
CANDLESTICK					
REVOLVER					
ROPE					
LEAD PIPE					
WRENCH					

ROOMS

HALL					
LOUNGE					
DINING ROOM					
KITCHEN					
BALL ROOM					
CONSERVATORY					
BILLIARDS ROOM					
LIBRARY					
STUDY					

CLUE SCORE SHEET

SUSPECTS

A.						
B.						
C.						
D.						
E.						
F.						

WEAPONS

KNIFE						
CANDLESTICK						
REVOLVER						
ROPE						
LEAD PIPE						
WRENCH						

ROOMS

HALL						
LOUNGE						
DINING ROOM						
KITCHEN						
BALL ROOM						
CONSERVATORY						
BILLIARDS ROOM						
LIBRARY						
STUDY						

CLUE SCORE SHEET

SUSPECTS

A.					
B.					
C.					
D.					
E.					
F.					

WEAPONS

KNIFE					
CANDLESTICK					
REVOLVER					
ROPE					
LEAD PIPE					
WRENCH					

ROOMS

HALL					
LOUNGE					
DINING ROOM					
KITCHEN					
BALL ROOM					
CONSERVATORY					
BILLIARDS ROOM					
LIBRARY					
STUDY					

CLUE SCORE SHEET

SUSPECTS

A.					
B.					
C.					
D.					
E.					
F.					

WEAPONS

KNIFE					
CANDLESTICK					
REVOLVER					
ROPE					
LEAD PIPE					
WRENCH					

ROOMS

HALL					
LOUNGE					
DINING ROOM					
KITCHEN					
BALL ROOM					
CONSERVATORY					
BILLIARDS ROOM					
LIBRARY					
STUDY					

CLUE SCORE SHEET

SUSPECTS

A.					
B.					
C.					
D.					
E.					
F.					

WEAPONS

KNIFE					
CANDLESTICK					
REVOLVER					
ROPE					
LEAD PIPE					
WRENCH					

ROOMS

HALL					
LOUNGE					
DINING ROOM					
KITCHEN					
BALL ROOM					
CONSERVATORY					
BILLIARDS ROOM					
LIBRARY					
STUDY					

CLUE SCORE SHEET

SUSPECTS

A.						
B.						
C.						
D.						
E.						
F.						

WEAPONS

KNIFE					
CANDLESTICK					
REVOLVER					
ROPE					
LEAD PIPE					
WRENCH					

ROOMS

HALL					
LOUNGE					
DINING ROOM					
KITCHEN					
BALL ROOM					
CONSERVATORY					
BILLIARDS ROOM					
LIBRARY					
STUDY					

CLUE SCORE SHEET

SUSPECTS

A.						
B.						
C.						
D.						
E.						
F.						

WEAPONS

KNIFE						
CANDLESTICK						
REVOLVER						
ROPE						
LEAD PIPE						
WRENCH						

ROOMS

HALL						
LOUNGE						
DINING ROOM						
KITCHEN						
BALL ROOM						
CONSERVATORY						
BILLIARDS ROOM						
LIBRARY						
STUDY						

CLUE SCORE SHEET

SUSPECTS

A.						
B.						
C.						
D.						
E.						
F.						

WEAPONS

KNIFE						
CANDLESTICK						
REVOLVER						
ROPE						
LEAD PIPE						
WRENCH						

ROOMS

HALL						
LOUNGE						
DINING ROOM						
KITCHEN						
BALL ROOM						
CONSERVATORY						
BILLIARDS ROOM						
LIBRARY						
STUDY						

CLUE SCORE SHEET

SUSPECTS

A.					
B.					
C.					
D.					
E.					
F.					

WEAPONS

KNIFE					
CANDLESTICK					
REVOLVER					
ROPE					
LEAD PIPE					
WRENCH					

ROOMS

HALL					
LOUNGE					
DINING ROOM					
KITCHEN					
BALL ROOM					
CONSERVATORY					
BILLIARDS ROOM					
LIBRARY					
STUDY					

CLUE SCORE SHEET

SUSPECTS

A.						
B.						
C.						
D.						
E.						
F.						

WEAPONS

KNIFE						
CANDLESTICK						
REVOLVER						
ROPE						
LEAD PIPE						
WRENCH						

ROOMS

HALL						
LOUNGE						
DINING ROOM						
KITCHEN						
BALL ROOM						
CONSERVATORY						
BILLIARDS ROOM						
LIBRARY						
STUDY						

CLUE SCORE SHEET

SUSPECTS

A.					
B.					
C.					
D.					
E.					
F.					

WEAPONS

KNIFE					
CANDLESTICK					
REVOLVER					
ROPE					
LEAD PIPE					
WRENCH					

ROOMS

HALL					
LOUNGE					
DINING ROOM					
KITCHEN					
BALL ROOM					
CONSERVATORY					
BILLIARDS ROOM					
LIBRARY					
STUDY					

CLUE SCORE SHEET

SUSPECTS

A.						
B.						
C.						
D.						
E.						
F.						

WEAPONS

KNIFE					
CANDLESTICK					
REVOLVER					
ROPE					
LEAD PIPE					
WRENCH					

ROOMS

HALL					
LOUNGE					
DINING ROOM					
KITCHEN					
BALL ROOM					
CONSERVATORY					
BILLIARDS ROOM					
LIBRARY					
STUDY					

CLUE SCORE SHEET

SUSPECTS

A.					
B.					
C.					
D.					
E.					
F.					

WEAPONS

KNIFE					
CANDLESTICK					
REVOLVER					
ROPE					
LEAD PIPE					
WRENCH					

ROOMS

HALL					
LOUNGE					
DINING ROOM					
KITCHEN					
BALL ROOM					
CONSERVATORY					
BILLIARDS ROOM					
LIBRARY					
STUDY					

CLUE SCORE SHEET

SUSPECTS

A.						
B.						
C.						
D.						
E.						
F.						

WEAPONS

KNIFE					
CANDLESTICK					
REVOLVER					
ROPE					
LEAD PIPE					
WRENCH					

ROOMS

HALL					
LOUNGE					
DINING ROOM					
KITCHEN					
BALL ROOM					
CONSERVATORY					
BILLIARDS ROOM					
LIBRARY					
STUDY					

CLUE SCORE SHEET

SUSPECTS

A.					
B.					
C.					
D.					
E.					
F.					

WEAPONS

KNIFE					
CANDLESTICK					
REVOLVER					
ROPE					
LEAD PIPE					
WRENCH					

ROOMS

HALL					
LOUNGE					
DINING ROOM					
KITCHEN					
BALL ROOM					
CONSERVATORY					
BILLIARDS ROOM					
LIBRARY					
STUDY					

CLUE SCORE SHEET

SUSPECTS

A.					
B.					
C.					
D.					
E.					
F.					

WEAPONS

KNIFE					
CANDLESTICK					
REVOLVER					
ROPE					
LEAD PIPE					
WRENCH					

ROOMS

HALL					
LOUNGE					
DINING ROOM					
KITCHEN					
BALL ROOM					
CONSERVATORY					
BILLIARDS ROOM					
LIBRARY					
STUDY					

CLUE SCORE SHEET

SUSPECTS

A.					
B.					
C.					
D.					
E.					
F.					

WEAPONS

KNIFE					
CANDLESTICK					
REVOLVER					
ROPE					
LEAD PIPE					
WRENCH					

ROOMS

HALL					
LOUNGE					
DINING ROOM					
KITCHEN					
BALL ROOM					
CONSERVATORY					
BILLIARDS ROOM					
LIBRARY					
STUDY					

CLUE SCORE SHEET

SUSPECTS

A.					
B.					
C.					
D.					
E.					
F.					

WEAPONS

KNIFE				
CANDLESTICK				
REVOLVER				
ROPE				
LEAD PIPE				
WRENCH				

ROOMS

HALL				
LOUNGE				
DINING ROOM				
KITCHEN				
BALL ROOM				
CONSERVATORY				
BILLIARDS ROOM				
LIBRARY				
STUDY				

CLUE SCORE SHEET

SUSPECTS

A.						
B.						
C.						
D.						
E.						
F.						

WEAPONS

KNIFE					
CANDLESTICK					
REVOLVER					
ROPE					
LEAD PIPE					
WRENCH					

ROOMS

HALL					
LOUNGE					
DINING ROOM					
KITCHEN					
BALL ROOM					
CONSERVATORY					
BILLIARDS ROOM					
LIBRARY					
STUDY					

CLUE SCORE SHEET

SUSPECTS

A.					
B.					
C.					
D.					
E.					
F.					

WEAPONS

KNIFE					
CANDLESTICK					
REVOLVER					
ROPE					
LEAD PIPE					
WRENCH					

ROOMS

HALL					
LOUNGE					
DINING ROOM					
KITCHEN					
BALL ROOM					
CONSERVATORY					
BILLIARDS ROOM					
LIBRARY					
STUDY					

CLUE SCORE SHEET

SUSPECTS

A.					
B.					
C.					
D.					
E.					
F.					

WEAPONS

KNIFE					
CANDLESTICK					
REVOLVER					
ROPE					
LEAD PIPE					
WRENCH					

ROOMS

HALL					
LOUNGE					
DINING ROOM					
KITCHEN					
BALL ROOM					
CONSERVATORY					
BILLIARDS ROOM					
LIBRARY					
STUDY					

CLUE SCORE SHEET

SUSPECTS

A.						
B.						
C.						
D.						
E.						
F.						

WEAPONS

KNIFE						
CANDLESTICK						
REVOLVER						
ROPE						
LEAD PIPE						
WRENCH						

ROOMS

HALL						
LOUNGE						
DINING ROOM						
KITCHEN						
BALL ROOM						
CONSERVATORY						
BILLIARDS ROOM						
LIBRARY						
STUDY						

CLUE SCORE SHEET

SUSPECTS

A.					
B.					
C.					
D.					
E.					
F.					

WEAPONS

KNIFE					
CANDLESTICK					
REVOLVER					
ROPE					
LEAD PIPE					
WRENCH					

ROOMS

HALL					
LOUNGE					
DINING ROOM					
KITCHEN					
BALL ROOM					
CONSERVATORY					
BILLIARDS ROOM					
LIBRARY					
STUDY					

CLUE SCORE SHEET

SUSPECTS

A.						
B.						
C.						
D.						
E.						
F.						

WEAPONS

KNIFE					
CANDLESTICK					
REVOLVER					
ROPE					
LEAD PIPE					
WRENCH					

ROOMS

HALL					
LOUNGE					
DINING ROOM					
KITCHEN					
BALL ROOM					
CONSERVATORY					
BILLIARDS ROOM					
LIBRARY					
STUDY					

CLUE SCORE SHEET

SUSPECTS

A.					
B.					
C.					
D.					
E.					
F.					

WEAPONS

KNIFE					
CANDLESTICK					
REVOLVER					
ROPE					
LEAD PIPE					
WRENCH					

ROOMS

HALL					
LOUNGE					
DINING ROOM					
KITCHEN					
BALL ROOM					
CONSERVATORY					
BILLIARDS ROOM					
LIBRARY					
STUDY					

CLUE SCORE SHEET

SUSPECTS

A.						
B.						
C.						
D.						
E.						
F.						

WEAPONS

KNIFE					
CANDLESTICK					
REVOLVER					
ROPE					
LEAD PIPE					
WRENCH					

ROOMS

HALL					
LOUNGE					
DINING ROOM					
KITCHEN					
BALL ROOM					
CONSERVATORY					
BILLIARDS ROOM					
LIBRARY					
STUDY					

CLUE SCORE SHEET

SUSPECTS

A.					
B.					
C.					
D.					
E.					
F.					

WEAPONS

KNIFE					
CANDLESTICK					
REVOLVER					
ROPE					
LEAD PIPE					
WRENCH					

ROOMS

HALL					
LOUNGE					
DINING ROOM					
KITCHEN					
BALL ROOM					
CONSERVATORY					
BILLIARDS ROOM					
LIBRARY					
STUDY					

CLUE SCORE SHEET

SUSPECTS

A.					
B.					
C.					
D.					
E.					
F.					

WEAPONS

KNIFE				
CANDLESTICK				
REVOLVER				
ROPE				
LEAD PIPE				
WRENCH				

ROOMS

HALL				
LOUNGE				
DINING ROOM				
KITCHEN				
BALL ROOM				
CONSERVATORY				
BILLIARDS ROOM				
LIBRARY				
STUDY				

CLUE SCORE SHEET

SUSPECTS

A.						
B.						
C.						
D.						
E.						
F.						

WEAPONS

KNIFE						
CANDLESTICK						
REVOLVER						
ROPE						
LEAD PIPE						
WRENCH						

ROOMS

HALL						
LOUNGE						
DINING ROOM						
KITCHEN						
BALL ROOM						
CONSERVATORY						
BILLIARDS ROOM						
LIBRARY						
STUDY						

CLUE SCORE SHEET

SUSPECTS

A.						
B.						
C.						
D.						
E.						
F.						

WEAPONS

KNIFE					
CANDLESTICK					
REVOLVER					
ROPE					
LEAD PIPE					
WRENCH					

ROOMS

HALL					
LOUNGE					
DINING ROOM					
KITCHEN					
BALL ROOM					
CONSERVATORY					
BILLIARDS ROOM					
LIBRARY					
STUDY					

CLUE SCORE SHEET

SUSPECTS

A.					
B.					
C.					
D.					
E.					
F.					

WEAPONS

KNIFE					
CANDLESTICK					
REVOLVER					
ROPE					
LEAD PIPE					
WRENCH					

ROOMS

HALL					
LOUNGE					
DINING ROOM					
KITCHEN					
BALL ROOM					
CONSERVATORY					
BILLIARDS ROOM					
LIBRARY					
STUDY					

CLUE SCORE SHEET

A.						
B.						
C.						
D.						
E.						
F.						

KNIFE					
CANDLESTICK					
REVOLVER					
ROPE					
LEAD PIPE					
WRENCH					

HALL					
LOUNGE					
DINING ROOM					
KITCHEN					
BALL ROOM					
CONSERVATORY					
BILLIARDS ROOM					
LIBRARY					
STUDY					

CLUE SCORE SHEET

SUSPECTS

A.					
B.					
C.					
D.					
E.					
F.					

WEAPONS

KNIFE					
CANDLESTICK					
REVOLVER					
ROPE					
LEAD PIPE					
WRENCH					

ROOMS

HALL					
LOUNGE					
DINING ROOM					
KITCHEN					
BALL ROOM					
CONSERVATORY					
BILLIARDS ROOM					
LIBRARY					
STUDY					

NOTES

NOTES

Made in the USA
Monee, IL
23 November 2020